MACHINES ★ AT WORK

GARBAGE TRUCKS

BY MARV ALINAS

THE CHILD'S WORLD® • MANKATO, MINNESOTA

The Child's World®

Published in the United States of America by The Child's World®
1980 Lookout Drive • Mankato, MN 56003-1705
800-599-READ • www.childsworld.com

PHOTO CREDITS

© David Hoffman Photo Library/Alamy: 7
© David M. Budd Photography: 16
© David R. Frazier Photolibrary, Inc./Alamy: 19
© Dennis MacDonald/Alamy: 4
© iStockphoto.com/Gautier Willaume: 12
© iStockphoto.com/Luis Carlos Torres: 15
© iStockphoto.com/Niilo Tippler: cover, 2, 11
© Jack Sullivan/Alamy: 8
© Rodolfo Arpia/Alamy: 20

ACKNOWLEDGMENTS

The Child's World®: Mary Berendes, Publishing Director;
Katherine Stevenson, Editor

The Design Lab: Kathleen Petelinsek, Design and Page Production

LIBRARY OF CONGRESS CATALOGING-IN-PUBLICATION DATA

Alinas, Marv.
  Garbage trucks / by Marv Alinas.
     p. cm. — (Machines at work)
  Includes bibliographical references and index.
  ISBN 1-59296-832-5 (library bound : alk. paper)
  1. Refuse collection vehicles—Juvenile literature. I. Title. II. Series.
  TD794.A435 2006
  628.4'42—dc22   2006023294

9/08

 Contents

This garbage truck is about to pick up someone's trash.

What are garbage trucks?

Garbage trucks are special kinds of **vehicles**. They carry trash away from homes and businesses. Garbage trucks are large. They can carry heavy loads.

How are garbage trucks used?

Garbage trucks carry lots of trash to **landfills**. They leave the trash at the landfill. Other machines push the trash into big piles. They cover the trash with dirt.

This machine is pushing trash into piles. Sometimes birds and other animals pick through the trash. They are looking for food to eat.

This machine is putting cans into piles. The cans will be recycled. The metal will be made into other things.

Not all trash is sent to landfills. Some trash can be used again. Finding new uses for trash is called **recycling**. Garbage trucks carry this trash to other places. There it is sorted. It will be sent away and used again.

What are the parts of a garbage truck?

In the front, garbage trucks look like other trucks. They have a **cab** where the driver sits. They have a large **engine**. The engine makes power that moves the wheels. The back of the truck has a big **box**. The box holds lots of garbage.

10

box

cab

This truck is a rear loader. The worker is dumping garbage into the box.

Are there different kinds of garbage trucks?

There are several kinds of garbage trucks. Rear loaders open at the back. The driver moves the truck slowly down the street. Garbage **collectors** hop on and off the back. They pick up garbage cans and trash bags. They throw the trash into the opening.

13

Other garbage trucks are front loaders. They have metal arms on the front. The arms pick up heavy trash bins. They lift the bins up and over the cab. The garbage falls into the top of the box. The arms lower the bins back down again.

★ This garbage truck is a front loader. It lifts the trash bin high over the box.

This garbage truck is a side loader.
The metal arm holds the garbage can.

Some garbage trucks are side loaders. They have a metal arm on the side. The driver stops by a garbage can. The arm lifts the can up high. It tips the can over. The trash falls into the box. The arm puts the can back down.

17

Recycling trucks have several bins. Garbage collectors sort the trash into the bins. They might put glass bottles in one bin. They might put cans in another.

18

This garbage collector is sorting trash. The blue bin holds paper. The paper will go in one opening. Cans will go in another opening.

This garbage truck is full of trash.
It is heading for the landfill. ⊛

Are garbage trucks helpful?

People need to get rid of their trash. Garbage trucks collect trash and carry it away. They keep our streets and cities clean. Garbage trucks are very helpful!

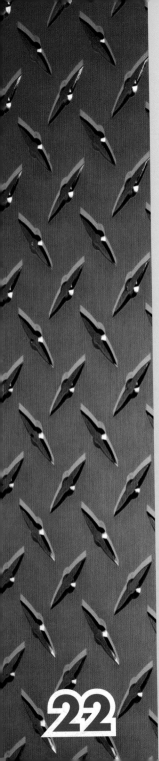

Glossary

box (BOX) A truck's box is the area in back where things are carried.

cab (KAB) A machine's cab is the area where the driver sits.

collectors (kuh-LEK-turz) Collectors are people who gather things.

engine (EN-jun) An engine is a machine that makes something move.

landfills (LAND-filz) Landfills are areas where towns put their garbage.

recycling (ree-SY-kling) Recycling is finding other uses for trash.

vehicles (VEE-uh-kullz) Vehicles are things for carrying people or goods.

 # Books

Brill, Marlene Targ. *Garbage Trucks.* Minneapolis: Lerner Publications, 2005.

Clark, Katie, and Amy Huntington (illustrator). *Grandma Drove the Garbage Truck.* Camden, ME: Down East Books, 2006.

Showers, Paul, and Randy Chewning (illustrator). *Where Does the Garbage Go?* New York: HarperCollins, 1994.

 # Web Sites

Visit our Web site for lots of links about garbage trucks:
http://www.childsworld.com/links

Note to parents, teachers, and librarians: We routinely check our Web links to make sure they're safe, active sites—so encourage your readers to check them out!

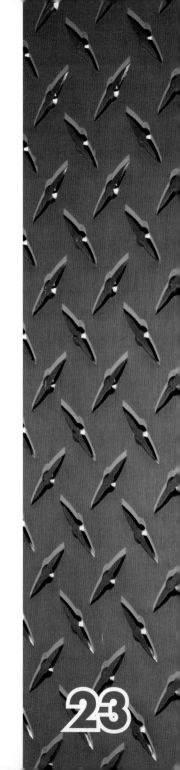

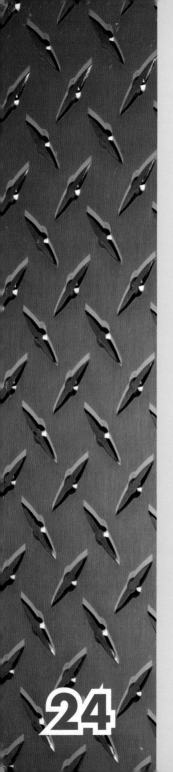

Index

About the Author

Marv Alinas has lived in Minnesota for over thirty years. When she's not reading or writing, Marv enjoys spending time with her dog and traveling to small river towns in northeastern Iowa and western Wisconsin.

24